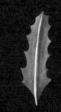

Easy Peasy: Gardening for Kids

Illustrated by Aitch
Written by Kirsten Bradley

This book was conceived, edited, and designed by gestalten.

Edited by Angela Francis and Robert Klanten

Design and layout by Constanze Hein, Book Book

Typefaces: Malaussène Translation by Laure Afchain, Berg by Andreas Johansen

Printed by Grafisches Centrum Cuno GmbH & Co. KG, Calbe (Saale)
Made in Germany

Published by Little Gestalten, Berlin 2019
ISBN 978-3-89955-824-1

For more information, and to order books, please visit www.little.gestalten.com.

Bibliographic information published by the Deutsche Nationalbibliothek.
The Deutsche Nationalbibliothek lists this publication in the Deutsche
Nationalbibliografie;

Detailed bibliographic data are available online at www.dnb.de.

This book was printed on paper certified according to the standards of the FSC®.

Easy Peasy

Gardening for Kids

LITTLE
GESTALTEN

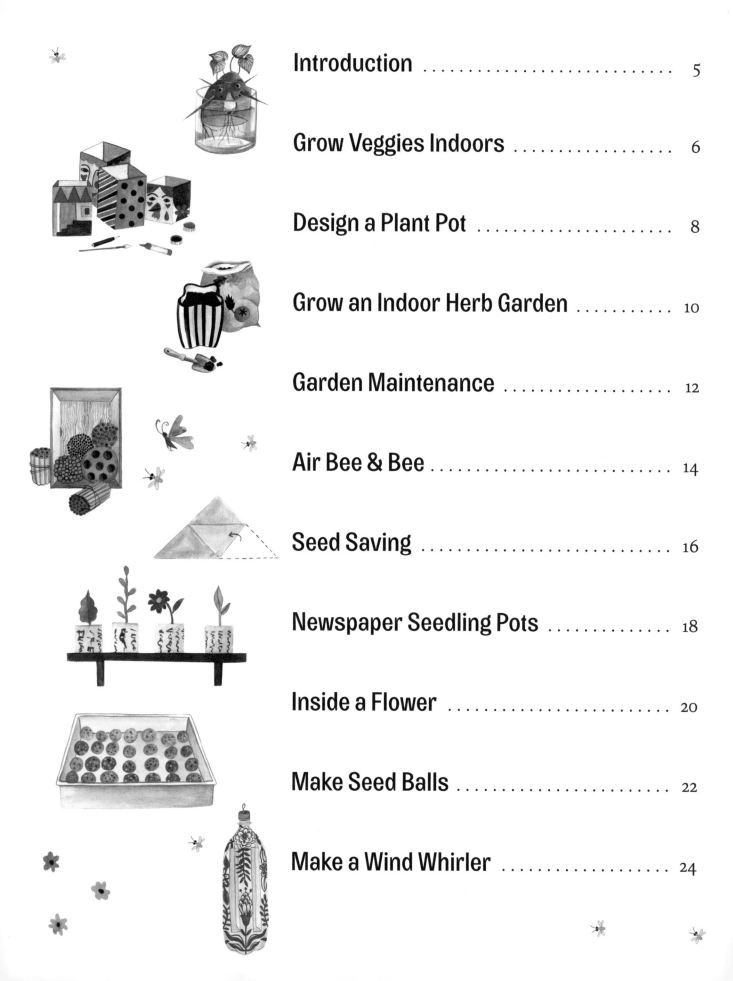

Introduction 5

Grow Veggies Indoors 6

Design a Plant Pot 8

Grow an Indoor Herb Garden 10

Garden Maintenance 12

Air Bee & Bee 14

Seed Saving 16

Newspaper Seedling Pots 18

Inside a Flower 20

Make Seed Balls 22

Make a Wind Whirler 24

Pollinator Pots 26

Keep a Wildlife Diary 28

Wildlife 30

Make a Kokedama 32

Feed the Birds 34

Make a Terrarium 36

Flower Friends 38

Press Flowers and Leaves 40

Grow a Peach Tree 42

Build a Bean Fort 44

Glossary 48

Growing a garden and caring for nature are for everyone! Whether you live in a house or an apartment, no matter if you have a small yard, a balcony, or even just a windowsill, you can still have a beautiful garden and learn about the ecosystem. All around you there are vegetables, plants, and flowers to grow, herbs you can add to your lunch, and nature to observe and learn about.

In these pages, you will find lots of projects to get you started growing, learning, observing, and doing. You could begin by making a pollinator pot or learning about the weather where you live, or you could make seed balls to grow flowers along your sidewalk. You could even grow new green friends from food scraps on your kitchen windowsill, like a sweet potato person. All of these projects are designed to be done by YOU, and most of them can be completed without the help of an adult.

Planting your own garden is fun and easy to do, and so is observing and learning about the ecosystem where you live. Keep a nature diary of the wildlife you see, press flowers that you find, or build an air bee and bee to attract pollinators to your back door.

Enjoy!

Grow Veggies Indoors

You Will Need

Toothpicks
Half a sweet potato
A glass of water
Spring onions
Soil

Did you know that some vegetables will regrow from kitchen scraps? And once they're grown, you can eat them all over again! All they need is a glass of water or a little soil.

2

Fill the glass with fresh water, leaving a few inches of space at the top.

1

Halfway up the sweet potato, stick a few toothpicks through. This will allow it to balance on the rim of the glass.

4

Put your sweet potato person somewhere with lots of light but no direct sun. It should start sprouting shoots with little leaves within a week. Make sure the bottom stays underwater at all times.

3

Place the sweet potato in the glass, with the cut part underwater and the uncut part above the water.

You can follow similar rules for spring onions in soil.

1

2

5 As the sweet potato grows, its vines will scramble up a window frame if you let them. The leaves are edible and can be used in salads or stews.

Design a Plant Pot

It's easy to make colorful flower pots for your plants!
Head to the kitchen to gather your materials, and remember
to save your empty cartons.

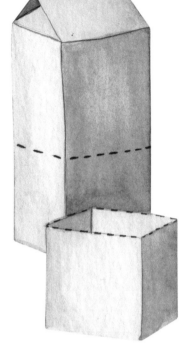

You Will Need

Plastic or waxed-paper milk cartons—empty and clean

One saucer per carton

A few flat pebbles

Scissors

Small plants

A marker pen

Potting mix

Paints and paint brushes

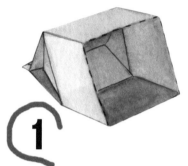

1 Take your empty carton and decide how tall you want your pot. Draw a line around the carton and cut. Throw the top part of the carton in your recycling can.

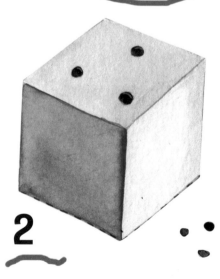

2 Poke three drainage holes in the base of your carton.

3 Now it's time to decorate! Use paints to make the sides of your carton bright with spots, stripes, or even faces.

4 ~~~ Half fill your carton with potting mix and add your small plant. Carefully add a little more soil until the carton is full, then press down firmly.

5 Cover the saucer with pebbles and place your carton on top.

You can also start flower seeds in this type of pot. Follow the growing instructions on page 26–27. Herbs work well too.

6 ~~ Lightly water, and enjoy your new flowerpot!

Grow an Indoor Herb Garden

Make a tasty garden inside your home by planting herbs on your windowsill. Before you start, decide where your herb garden will be—a sunny place is best!

You Will Need

A window box or several pots

A saucer or tray to sit underneath your pot

Potting mix

Fennel and parsley seeds

1

Fill your pot with soil, leaving five centimeters of space at the top. Press down firmly.

2

Take your fennel seeds and sprinkle them across half the surface of the soil.

3

Take your parsley seeds and sprinkle them across the other half of the soil.

4

Sprinkle soil over the seeds until they are just covered. Press down firmly.

The herbs will keep growing for a season or two if watered regularly.

5

Once your fennel and parsley is 15 centimeters high, you can start to harvest it, a little at a time. Use scissors so you don't disturb the roots.

Garden Maintenance

Soil
Soil is a plant's home, just like your house is your home. It's important to make sure this home is healthy and happy so your plants will be healthy and happy too. All soil types love the same thing—life!

Watering
A fun way to check if your garden needs watering is to stick your finger into the soil. Does it feel damp? Or does it feel dry and crumbly?

Compost
Adding compost to your soil is like giving it a big, nutritious meal so your plants can grow big and strong. To make compost, layer leaves, straw, or dry grass with nutritious things, like food scraps or freshly cut grass. Make lots of layers, like a lasagne. Your compost pile may get warm, and you may see steam rising off the top!

Air Bee & Bee

An easy way of attracting friendly bugs is to give them somewhere nice to stay! Many useful insects need a place to sleep that's dry and snug. You can help them by making an insect hotel. Different insects like different kinds of holes to sleep in.

You Will Need

An old but sturdy box made of wood, cardboard, or plastic

Short bundles of sticks, reeds, or thin bamboo

Thin wire

Pruning shears

Clay

Some insects like the nooks between sticks, some like the holes in reeds, and some like holes in mud or clay. Try to give the insects lots of different types of rooms to stay in!

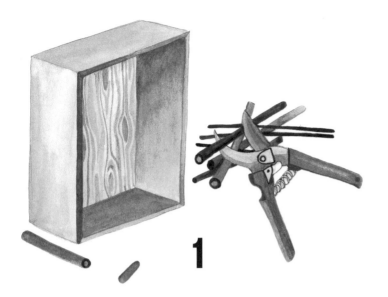

2

Mold the clay into a circle. Get a small stick and carefully poke holes into one side of the clay. Each hole should be at least five centimeters deep.

1

Put your box on its side. Measure the sticks and reeds so that they poke out of the box a little. Cut your sticks to size with pruning shears.

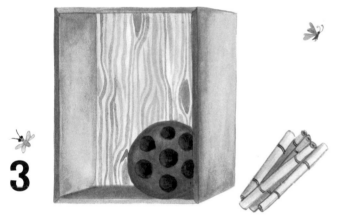

4

Bundle up your sticks and reeds, making sure to group together the same material, and then tie the sticks together firmly. Arrange the bundles of sticks in the box.

3

Put your clay shape in a corner of the box with the holes facing outward.

5 Carefully place your insect hotel outside, at least one meter off the ground. Put it in a sheltered place out of the rain, like on a shelf or table.

It will take a little while for insects to discover your hotel and check in, but one day you will notice that some of the holes have visitors. Some holes may even get completely covered over with insect guests, as they will tell their friends about the great new hotel they have found!

Seed Saving

If you save seeds from your plants, you can grow your favorite plants again and again. You can also share your seeds with all of your friends!

You Will Need

Square paper

1 Place the paper in front of you in a diamond shape.

2 Fold the bottom half up to meet the top half.

3 Take the bottom right corner and fold it up until it's top edge is straight.

4 Make sure it meets the other side of the paper.

5 Repeat with the left corner. Both corners should meet at the other side of the paper, with straight top edges.

6 Tuck the front layer of the top into the fold from step five.

16

You now have a seed envelope! Label, decorate, and fill it with seeds. To close the envelope, tuck the back layer of the top into the pocket. To best store your seeds, keep them somewhere cool, dry, and free of pests.

Newspaper Seedling Pots

You Will Need

Newspaper

Scissors

Scotch tape

An unopened can or a small bottle

It's easy to sprout your seeds in spring with newspaper seedling pots! First, construct seedling pots from old newspaper, and then once your seeds have sprouted, you can put the newspaper pots right into your garden, where the seedlings will take root.

1

Take two double sheets of newspaper and fold them over to create four layers of paper.

2

Cut the newspaper into three equal pieces, lengthwise. This will give you enough paper for three small pots.

3

Lay one set of newspaper strips in front of you lengthways, and place your can crosswise on the strip. Leave a three-centimeter section of paper at the end.

4

Loosely roll your can forward with the paper held against it, creating a tube of paper. Secure the end with scotch tape.

5

Fold the loose paper onto the bottom of the can to create the base of your pot. Squish it down tightly.

6

Twist the pot to remove the can, and start making another seedling pot!

While these pots may seem delicate, once they're full of soil and seeds, and all together and snug in a tray, they are remarkably strong.

7

Now place your seedling pots together on a tray and fill them with seed-raising mix. When it's time to plant them in your garden, simply remove the pieces of scotch tape and plant the whole pots!

Inside a Flower

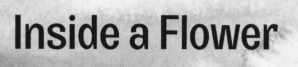

What Is Pollination?

Did you know that your garden depends on pollination? This is what happens when pollen is transferred between flowers—an exchange that makes flowers produce fruit and seeds.

How Does Pollination Occur?

First, pollen on the anthers (1) of a flower makes its way into the flower's stigma (2).

Pollen then travels down the pollen tube to fertilize the ovules inside the flower's ovary (3).

Then, slowly the fertilized ovary swells and becomes a fruit full of seeds. Depending on the plant species, this fruit may be a pear, a pumpkin, or a rose hip. Any fruit will contain fertilized seeds that can later be planted to grow another generation of plants.

Who Are the Pollinators?

To ensure pollination occurs, some types of plants need help to transport pollen from the male flowers to the female flowers. This is where pollinators can help!

Where Are the Pollinators?

Pollinators are all around us, every day. Some prefer specific types of plants, and some don't mind at all.

Wind moves pollen from flower to flower.
Bees visit multiple flowers to gather nectar and pollen, spreading pollen as they go.
Wasps also gather nectar and pollen, helping along the way.
Small birds drink the flowers' nectar, spreading pollen in the process.
Butterflies sip nectar here and there, carrying pollen on their legs and heads.
Moths visit and sip nectar from some special flowers that open at night.

Make Seed Balls

A seed ball is like a magical ball that you can use to grow flowers anywhere! It's a hard, dry ball of clay and compost with flower seeds in it. You can put your seed ball anywhere you like—then just wait for rain. When a big rainstorm comes, the water melts the clay and releases the seeds into the ground. In a month or two, you will get a burst of new flowers. And don't forget, more flowers also means more food for pollinators!

You Will Need

Powdered or modeling clay

Compost

A kitchen sieve

A bucket

A jug of water

Flower seeds

1 Sieve your compost into your bucket, as it needs to be very fine. Put the big leftover bits on your garden.

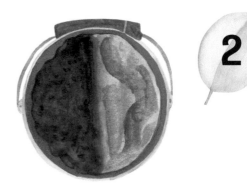

2 Add an equal amount of clay to the bucket so you have a half-clay, half-compost mix. If you're using modeling clay, squish it up first with a little water—just enough to make it soft.

3 Add your flower seeds to the bucket. One handful of seeds for two cups of the clay-compost mix is good, but you can use as little or as many seeds as you like.

4 Mix all the ingredients around and add little splashes of water until the mix is sticky enough to roll into balls.

5 Take a small portion of the mix and roll it into a ball between your hands. A ball about the size of a cherry is good! Put the ball on a tray to dry, and then repeat. The seed balls will store for many months.

6 Place or throw the seed balls where you would like flowers to grow. Be mindful of the season. Wait for rain and cross your fingers!

Make a Wind Whirler

Where does the wind where you live come from? Does it come from the east in spring and the west in autumn? Explore the weather in your garden and learn more about your ecosystem. This wind whirler is made out of a round plastic soda bottle. If you like, paint it bright colors!

You Will Need

A plastic bottle

Sharp scissors

A marker pen

A paper clip

String

1

Draw vertical lines down the body of your bottle, leaving space at the top and bottom. Leave a few fingers gap between each line.

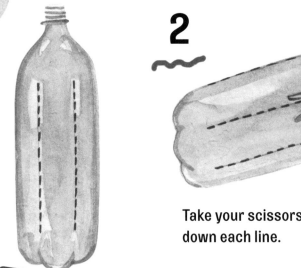

2

Take your scissors and carefully cut down each line.

3

At the top and bottom of each slit, make little horizontal cuts, always in the same direction.

4

Gently push each flap into the bottle a little. Repeat until each flap is pushed into the bottle.

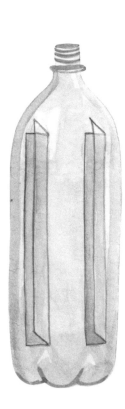

5

Now make a hole in your bottle lid and insert one end of your paper clip—bend it over so it can't come back through but can still turn freely.

With some string, hang your whirler up from a tree or balcony, somewhere it can twirl freely. Watch it whirl! You will soon learn where the wind comes from in your garden.

6

Decorate your wind whirler.

Pollinator Pots

To help attract pollinators like bees and butterflies to your garden, you can grow a pollinator pot. Pollinators will love these beautiful flowers, and so will you!

1

Find a position for your big pot before you begin, because once it's full, it will be heavy. Add some pebbles to the bottom of your pot. This will help the soil drain. Then add soil, leaving a 10-centimeter space at the top.

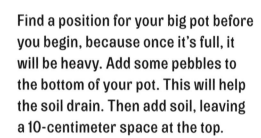

2 Sprinkle you flower seeds across the surface of your potting mix.

3 Sprinkle a little more potting mix to cover the seeds and pat down the soil firmly.

4 Water your pot regularly and watch the seeds emerge. Look out for pollinators and record which ones you see!

Pollinators to watch out for: bees, wasps, ladybugs, small birds, and butterflies.

Keep a Wildlife Diary

Keeping a wildlife diary for your garden is a great way to get to know the seasons, your garden, and the wildlife around you.

When we keep a diary, we often notice more things because we look for new things to write down. And the more you notice in your garden, the more you will understand it, year by year. You may be surprised at what you see!

You can organize your diary by month or by season. Use a blank book, and at the top clearly write the date and where you are. Now note down everything that you notice in your garden.

You can record things like which varieties of vegetables you plant and which ones you liked eating the most. You can also add pressed flowers and leaves to your nature diary so you remember which ones were your favorites.

Things to Look out For:

Which flowers come out first in spring?
Which flowers last the longest?

Who visits the blue flowers the most?
Is it ladybugs, bees, or butterflies?

What spider species do you have in
your garden? Look them up and learn
their names.

Which day of spring did the first
leaves come out on the big tree?
Which day of autumn did the tree
lose its last leaves?

When did you plant your
beans this year?
And when did you pick
your final harvest?

What kinds of clouds
can you see?
Look up the different types
and learn their names.

Where do the snails like to live in your garden?
Do you have any frogs?

Wildlife

What insects can you find in your garden? Take a magnifying glass with you and have a good look. Peer inside flowers and check out their leaves, and look under rocks, bricks, and into all the little hidden holes that insects love. Trees are also a good place to look because there's so much life living inside them. For example, you might find bugs and spiders living inside the bark, or even animals and birds living in tree hollows!

Look out for:

Spider

Millipede

Dragonfly

Cockchafer

Butterfly

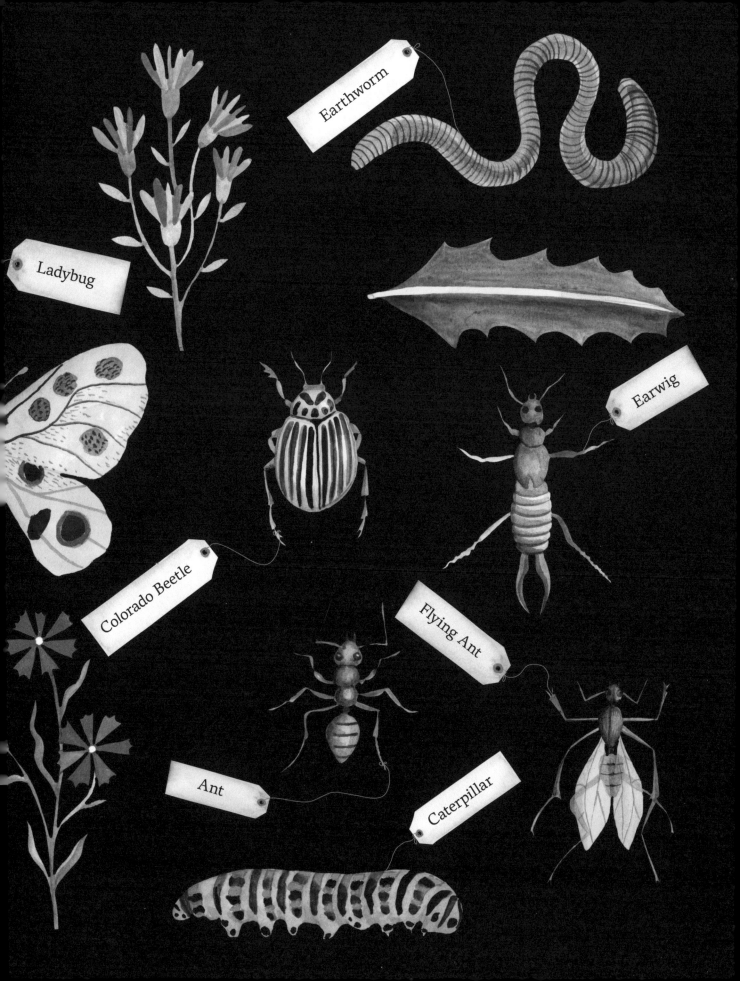

Make a Kokedama

No spare windowsill to put a pot?
No problem. You can make a fuzzy
kokedama that hangs inside, bringing
a touch of green to your home.

You Will Need

Potting mix   Sand

Two 30-square-centimeter
pieces of burlap

Lots of string   A small fern

Fresh moss

1

Mix two handfuls of soil and
two handfuls of sand together
in a bucket.

2

Cut two one-meter pieces of string and
lay them on a table in an X shape.

3

Lay your piece of burlap on top of the
string, in the middle of the X, and place the
soil-sand mix in the middle of the burlap.

4

Gently remove your plant from its pot,
leaving a little soil on the roots. Place
it in the middle of the pile of soil-sand mix.

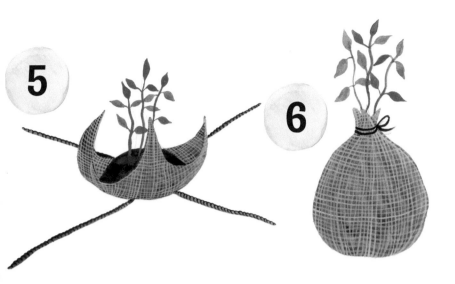

5 Carefully lift up the corners of the burlap to make a pocket with the soil inside and the plant poking out the top. Use the string and wrap the burlap to form a rough ball.

6 Wrap the second piece of burlap around the ball and tie to secure at the top.

7 Now take your moss and put it onto the ball. Secure it with more string.

8 Wrap up the kokedama with as much string as you like until it's a firm ball.

9 Then, soak it! Put your kokedama in a bowl of water and leave it for 30 minutes.

Soak your kokedama every few weeks, or when the outside feels very dry.

10 Drain your kokedama until it stops dripping (the bath or shower is a good place to do this) and hang it up!

Feed the Birds

In early spring, there can be very little food for small birds to eat. Birds are an important part of our gardens and ecosystems, so making a feeder to provide them with tasty food can help them stay healthy. This is a good project to do in winter so you're ready for spring.

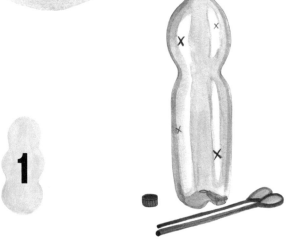

1

Mark where the perches on the feeder will go, with a dot on each side of the bottle for each perch. It's good to have them crossways from each other and at different heights.

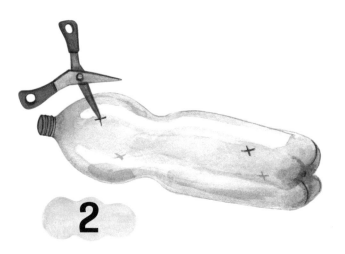

2

With the help of an adult, carefully punch holes with your scissors where you made the marks. It's fine if the holes split a bit.

3

Push your spoons through your perch holes, right up to the spoon ends. The spoons should be firm so they don't fall out but still have room to wiggle.

4

Put your funnel in the top of the bottle and pour in the birdseed until the bottle is nearly full.

34

5 Tightly screw the cap on your bottle, and use the wire and string to hang your feeder.

As little birds visit your feeder and sit on the spoons, their weight will jiggle the perches, releasing a little food for them to eat. When the seed level in the bottle goes below the bottom perch, and the birds cannot get any more food, simply take your feeder down and fill it back up!

Make a Terrarium

Bring the garden inside with a terrarium!
A terrarium works a bit like an ecosystem.
Inside the jar is a small world. The relationship
between your plants and the warmth and
moisture they create inside the jar keeps
them healthy. You can even keep the
terrarium next to your bed so that nature
is the first thing you see when you wake
up in the morning!

You Will Need

A jar

Small plants that like
shade—ferns and
succulents work well

Fresh moss

Activated charcoal

Soil

Sand

 1

Place charcoal in the bottom of your jar, enough to cover the base.

 **2**

Mix equal parts soil and sand in a bucket. Add to the jar until the jar is ⅓ full.

 **3**

Carefully remove your plants from their pots and shake the soil off their roots. Place them into the jar with their roots spread out.

4

Carefully place moss all around the plants until the entire surface is covered with moss. Press down firmly and then water your plants.

5

Place your terrarium wherever you like in your room, as long as it's out of direct sunlight. Water your terrarium sparingly, just a little at a time.

Tip: talk to your terrarium! When you breathe out, you are expelling the carbon dioxide that plants need to grow. Talking to your terrarium will help keep it healthy.

Flower Friends

Did you know that some plants like living together and some plants do not? Some plants grow stronger and bigger when placed next to each other and others don't. Planting friends together is called "companion planting." Planting some vegetables next to each other can even make them taste better!

When harvesting green things like spinach or herbs, snip the leaves off with garden scissors so that you don't damage the roots by pulling out part of the plant. This will allow the leaves to grow back, which means more food! But when harvesting things like carrots or radishes, pull out the whole plant. Try to make sure the soil on them falls onto the garden, not your kitchen sink or floor!

Press Flowers and Leaves

You Will Need

A big book

Newspaper

A weight (a brick will do)

Flowers to press

Pressed flowers and leaves can be used for arts and crafts all year long! Some are better for pressing than others. A flower or leaf will be good for pressing if it has a flattish face and no big bumpy bits in it. Things like pansies, small daisies, nigella, or autumn leaves work well. For bigger flowers, you can remove the petals and just press them.

1 Open your book and lay a piece of newspaper on the page.

2 Arrange your flowers on the newspaper so they are as flat as possible.

3 Cover them with another piece of newspaper and close the book carefully.

4 Place a weight on the book to help press the flowers.

40

5 Wait a month, then take a peek! If your flowers are not completely dry, press them for another month.

Grow a Peach Tree

You Will Need

Clean and dry peach stones

Somewhere cold to store them until spring

A jar with a lid

Small pots filled with compost

Have you ever wondered how a peach stone turns into a peach tree? Plant your own so you can see...

1

After eating your yummiest peaches, gather the stones together. Put them in a jar in the fridge until early spring.

In spring, carefully transfer each stone to a small pot of compost. If one or two have already sprouted, that is fine, just plant them with the roots facing down.

Place your seedling pots somewhere warm and keep them damp.

Once your peach seedling is growing well, you can transfer it to a larger pot.

When your peach tree becomes a sapling, plant it outside and cross your fingers for many peaches. The tree will start fruiting in three to four years.

Peaches do not grow "true to type," which means the fruit on the new tree may not be the same as the peaches you ate to get the seed.

Build a Bean Fort

You Will Need

Lots of climbing/ runner bean seeds (check that they're climbers, not bush beans)

A trowel

Sturdy string or wire

Lots of long sticks, at least two meters long

Build your own living fort in the garden! Then you can hide inside with plenty of yummy snacks. If you don't have a garden, try planting beans in a pot and making the vines grow around a window.

1

Find a sunny spot for your fort. Mark out a circle on the ground and dig a trench around the circle's edge, about 10 centimeters deep.

2

Take your long sticks and prop them up in a tepee-like structure, with their bases in your trench. Get an adult to help hold them at the top.

3

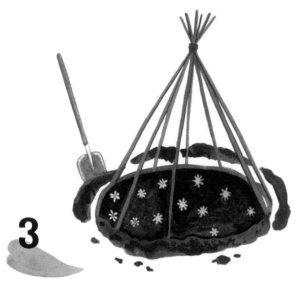

Tie the sticks together firmly at the top with your string or wire. Make sure you've left a gap for a doorway in the fort.

4

Fill the trench with the soil you've removed to secure the bases of the sticks. Leave the soil loose, as this is where you'll plant your beans.

5

Now that your fort is built, plant your bean seeds all the way around your trench, except for the doorway. Plant them one thumb length deep and cover with more soil.

6

Water your seeds once. Don't water them again until the seedlings emerge (within seven days).

Watch your beans wind their way up the poles as they grow! Soon you will have a green bean fort that you can sit inside, where you can eat beans all day.

Glossary

Anthers
The anthers in a flower contain pollen. You can find the anthers by looking inside a flower, like a tulip, and finding the long, thin stalks. The tops of the stalks are round—these are the anthers.

Burlap
A rough, natural woven fabric that can be used for gardening.

Clay
A thick, sticky form of soil that can be molded when it's wet and then dried— to make pottery or bricks, for example.

Compost
A mixture of decomposing food scraps that is added to soil to fertilize and improve it. This gives plants more nutrients to help them grow.

Concrete
A strong, heavy material that is made up of a mixture of stone, gravel, cement, sand, and water. Concrete is used to make roads and buildings.

Fennel
A herb that tastes like licorice and is used for cooking and making tea.

Fern
A plant that grows large feathery leaves and does not flower. Many ferns can thrive in places that do not have much light, like the forest.

Fertilization
When the male and female reproductive cells join together to create a new plant, fertilization occurs. Another meaning of fertilization is the improvement of the quality of soil by adding compost or other material that helps plants grow.

Harvest
When you pick vegetables and fruits that are ready to eat.

Kokedama
A ball of soil covered with moss from which a plant grows. You can hang your kokedama up, or place it on a tray.

Loam
A type of soil made of clay and sand that is good for growing plants.

Nigella
A species of flowering plants that are often blue, pink, or white.

Ovary
The female reproductive organ inside a flower.

Pansy
A small garden flower that has round petals and comes in many colors.

Pollen
The fine powder inside a flower that comes from the male reproductive organ. Pollen can fertilize another flower, or even the same flower, when it meets the female reproductive organ in that flower.

Pollinators
Anything that helps a flower spread its pollen, like insects, birds, or the wind.

Pollination
This is when pollen is transferred between the male and female parts of a flower.

Sapling
A young tree with a thin trunk that will grow into an adult tree.

Seed
A tiny grain that contains the beginning of a new plant.

Stigma
The part of a flower that receives pollen from other plants, this is where pollen grains germinate. Inside a flower, like a daffodil, there are tiny stalks. In the middle is one bigger and taller stalk—this is the stigma.

Succulent
A thick and fleshy plant that grows in dry areas and stores water in its leaves.

Trowel
A small handheld tool that can be used for digging holes while gardening.